A Beginning-to-Read Book

T0021324

BIG FEELINGS
FEELING JOYFUL

by Mary Lindeen

NORWOOD HOUSE PRESS

DEAR CAREGIVER, The *Beginning to Read* Big Feelings books support children's social and emotional learning (SEL). SEL has been proven to promote not only the development of self-awareness, responsibility, and positive relationships but also academic achievement.

Current research reveals that the part of the brain that manages emotion is directly connected to the part of the brain that is used in cognitive tasks such as problem solving, logic, reasoning, and critical thinking—all of which are at the heart of learning.

SEL is also directly linked to what are referred to as 21st Century Skills: collaboration, communication, creativity, and critical thinking. The books included in this SEL series offer an early start to help children build the competencies they need for success in school and life.

In each of these books, young children will learn how to recognize, name, and manage their own feelings while learning that everyone shares the same emotions. This helps them develop social competencies that will benefit them in their relationships with others, which in turn contributes to their success in school. As they read, children will also practice early reading skills by reading sight words and content vocabulary.

The reinforcements in the back of each book will help you determine how well your child understands the concepts in the book, provide different ideas for your child to practice fluency, and suggest books and websites for additional reading.

The most important part of the reading experience with these books—and all others—is for your child to have fun and enjoy reading and learning!

Sincerely,

Mary Lindeen

Mary Lindeen, Author

Norwood House Press
For more information about Norwood House Press please visit our website at www.norwoodhousepress.com or call 866-565-2900.
© 2022 Norwood House Press. Beginning-to-Read™ is a trademark of Norwood House Press.
All rights reserved. No part of this book may be reproduced or utilized in any form or
by any means without written permission from the publisher.

Editor: Judy Kentor Schmauss **Designer:** Sara Radka

Photo Credits: Getty Images: 10'000 Hours, 21, Camille Tokerud, 22, Digital Vision, cover, 1, EyeEm/Anastasiya Stoeva, 17, Hill Street Studios, 18, Jacobs Stock Photography Ltd, 10, Jose Luis Pelaez Inc, 14, kate_sept2004, 9, Klaus Vedfelt, 26, martin-dm, 25, PeopleImages, 3, praetorianphoto, 5, Russell Monk, 29, sarahwolfephotography, 13, Westend61, 6

Library of Congress Cataloging-in-Publication Data has been filed and is available at catalog.loc.gov

Library ISBN: 978-1-68450-823-5   Paperback ISBN: 978-1-68404-665-2

Feeling joyful comes from paying attention to the goodness around you.

Everyone can find something to feel joyful about.

But different people find joy in different things.

What makes you feel joyful?

Is it listening to music?

Maybe it's spending time outside.

Maybe you feel joyful when you're with family or friends.

Or you feel joyful when you're making or building something.

Earning something you've worked hard for can make you feel joyful.

Helping others makes many people feel joyful.

It's not always
easy to feel joyful.

And no one feels
joyful all the time.

But there are things you can do to feel joyful more often.

You can choose to notice the world around you.

Look for beautiful or interesting things.

Find ways to
help others.

Thank people
who help you.

Take time each day to think about the people and things that made your day better.

Find reasons to laugh!

Laughing is one way to show you're feeling joyful.

Smiling is another
way to show your joy.

Sometimes
your whole body
shows that you're
feeling joyful!

But sometimes joyful feelings are on the inside.

You feel quietly calm, peaceful, and thankful.

What can you do to feel joyful today?

... READING REINFORCEMENT...

CONNECTING CONCEPTS

CLOSE READING OF NONFICTION TEXT

Close reading helps children comprehend text. It includes reading a text, discussing it with others, and answering questions about it. Use these questions to discuss this book with your child:

1. What does it mean to feel joyful?

2. What are some things a person can do to feel joyful more often?

Once you have discussed the above questions, ask your child to either draw a picture of someone who is feeling joyful or choose one of the children pictured in the book. Then ask the following questions about the child in the drawing or the photo:

1. How can you tell this person might be feeling joyful?

2. What might be one reason this person is feeling joyful?

3. How would you feel in that situation?

4. Do you ever feel joyful? When?

5. How do you show that you're feeling joyful?

VOCABULARY AND LANGUAGE SKILLS

As you read the book with your child, make sure he or she understands the vocabulary used. Point to key words and talk about what they mean. Encourage children to sound out new words or to read the familiar words around an unfamiliar word for help reading new words.

FLUENCY

Help your child practice fluency by using one or more of the following activities:

1. Reread the book to your child at least two times while he or she uses a finger to track each word as it is read.

2. Read a line of the book, then reread it as your child reads along with you.

3. Ask your child to go back through the book and read the words he or she knows.

4. Have your child practice reading the book several times to improve accuracy, rate, and expression.

FURTHER READING FOR KIDS

Gee, Kimberly. *Glad, Glad Bear!* New York, NY: Beach Lane Books, 2020.

Raczka, Robert. *Niko Draws a Feeling.* Minneapolis, MN: Carolrhoda Books, 2017.

Sesame Workshop. *Just One You! A Joyful Celebration of the Differences That Make Us All Special.* Naperville, IL: Sourcebooks LLC, 2021.

FURTHER READING FOR TEACHERS/CAREGIVERS

Aha! Parenting: Teaching Your Child the Art of Happiness
https://www.ahaparenting.com/parenting-tools/emotional-intelligence/happiness

Greater Good Magazine: How to Awaken Joy in Kids
https://greatergood.berkeley.edu/article/item/how_to_awaken_joy_in_kids

Tinkergarten: 5 Reasons to Help Kids Seek Joy Right Now
https://tinkergarten.com/blog/how-joy-helps-kids-thrive

Word List

Feeling Joyful uses the 91 words listed below. *High-frequency* words are those words that are used most often in the English language. They are sometimes referred to as sight words because children need to learn to recognize them automatically when they read. *Content* words are any words specific to a particular topic. Regular practice reading these words will enhance your child's ability to read with greater fluency and comprehension.

HIGH-FREQUENCY WORDS

about	find	no	things
all	for	not	think
always	from	often	time
and	good(ness)	on	to
another	help(ing)	one	way(s)
are	in	or	what
around	is	other(s)	when
but	it	people	who
can	look	show(s)	with
come(s)	made	something	work(ed)
day	make(s)	take	world
different	making	that	you
do	many	the	your
each	more	there	

CONTENT WORDS

attention	everyone	laugh(ing)	reasons
beautiful	family	listening	smiling
better	feel(ing, ings, s)	maybe	sometimes
body	friends	music	spending
building	hard	notice	thank(ful)
calm	inside	outside	today
choose	interesting	paying	whole
earning	it's	peaceful	you're
easy	joy(ful)	quietly	you've

About the Author

Mary Lindeen is a writer, editor, parent, and former elementary school teacher. She has written mo[...] 100 books for children and edited many more. She specializes in early literacy instruction and book[...] readers, especially nonfiction.